MW00364987

50
WAYS TO
CLOSE
A SALE

50
WAYS TO
CLOSE
A SALE
(And Keep the Customer for Life)

☆

GERALD
MICHAELSON

WILLIAM MORROW AND COMPANY, INC.
New York

It is the policy of William Morrow and Company, Inc., and its imprints and affiliates, recognizing the importance of preserving what has been written, to print the books we publish on acid-free paper, and we exert our best efforts to that end.

Library of Congress Cataloging-in-Publication Data

Michaelson, Gerald A.
    50 ways to close a sale (and keep the customer for life) / by Gerald Michaelson.
        p.   cm.
    ISBN 0-688-11567-5
    1. Selling.   2. Consumer satisfaction. 3. Consumers' preferences.   I. Title.   II. Title: Fifty ways to close a sale (and keep the customer for life)
HF5438.25.M537   1994
658.85—dc20   94-7519
                                                        CIP

Printed in the United States of America

First Edition

1   2   3   4   5   6   7   8   9   10

BOOK DESIGN BY MICHAEL MENDELSOHN/MM DESIGN 2000, INC.

To Jan, with love—
thanks for the support
during the many times
I've been out of town.

ACKNOWLEDGMENTS

With thanks:

To the customers, sales professionals, and managers with whom I have been privileged to work and from whom I have learned so much.

To the many helpful friends I've met along my career path at Maytag, Magnavox, Philips Electronics, Abt Associates, and Tennessee Associates International.

To Steve Rivkin who introduced me to Barry Tarshis and John Boswell—who gave their expert assistance in developing the content.

CONTENTS

Part V   Making the Customer Your Partner 109

PART I

SELLING THEN AND NOW

Reflections on the Process

☆

1

THE GOSPEL ACCORDING
TO DALE CARNEGIE

THE MOST INFLUENTIAL BOOK ON SELLING ever written is Dale Carnegie's *How to Win Friends and Influence People*. Originally published in 1937 and updated in 1981 by Carnegie's wife, it is a gold mine of timeless advice on how to win people over without resorting to deceit or blatant manipulation, and it is one of those rare books that anybody who wants to be successful in sales should read not just once, but over and over.

The basic sales lesson in Carnegie's book can be summed up very simply: Do everything in your power to make the people you are hoping to sell feel appreciated and important, and they will become your customers. Treat the people who are already buying from you the same way, and they will remain your customers for life.

Carnegie continually reminds you throughout the book that the only way to win in the dealings you have with other people is to subordinate your own needs, desires, and impulses to those of the other person. But he is quick to caution that your concern for other people has to be *genuine*. Otherwise, people will see through it, and the strategy will backfire.

The world has changed a great deal, of course, since Carnegie's book first appeared; and the sales profession, as I will be stressing over the next few pages, has changed quite a bit as well. Even so, the core message of Carnegie's book remains as valid today as it was nearly sixty years ago. What follows are six Carnegie pearls that I have found especially valuable throughout the thirty years I have been selling.

1 **The "Big Secret" of Dealing with People** "Give honest and sincere appreciation."

2 **How to Get People to Do What You Want Them to Do** "The only way on earth to influence other people is to talk about what *they* want and show them how to get it."

3 **Getting People to Like You** "Become genuinely interested in other people. Smile. Be a good listener. Talk in terms of the other person's interests. Make the other person feel important."

4 **The Only Way to Get the Best of an Argument** "Avoid it."

5 **The Best Thing to Do When You're Wrong** "Admit it quickly and emphatically."

6 **On the Importance of Serving** "The world is full of people who are grabbing and self-seeking. So the rare individual who unselfishly tries to serve others has an enormous advantage. He has little competition."

WHAT DALE CARNEGIE LEFT OUT

A S INVALUABLE A SELLING PRIMER AS *How to Win Friends and Influence People* may be, its principles need to be adapted to the modern world and to the changes that have been taking place in the selling profession itself. Two of these changes are far-reaching enough that they deserve special mention:

The Advent of Team Selling In Carnegie's time, your success in sales depended mainly on your one-on-one skills—that is, on the personal attributes you were able to bring to each selling situation, and on the relationship you were able to establish with your prospects and customers.

One-on-one skills and personal relationships are still important in sales, but most salespeople today no longer operate as Lone Rangers in the field. They perform instead as key members of a selling team. Their collective goal is to generate the value-added service that wins and maintains the loyalty of the customer.

If you sell cars for a living, for instance, you probably work closely with your showroom manager, with the service department of your dealership, and with the specialist in your dealership who handles leasing and financing. Everyone collaborates to exert a team effort. If you sell sophisticated information services, you must routinely include as part of your sales effort the input from your company's software and hardware experts. You coordinate their recommendations not only with the buyer but with the technical specialists in the buyer's company.

Even if you sell clothing in a retail store, there's a good chance that other people—the store manager, people in the tailoring department, people in the credit and shipping departments—also contribute to the effort of keeping your customers happy.

What this basic shift in the selling paradigm means to you as a sales professional is this: You spend less of your time "selling" today in the old-fashioned sense of the word and more time facilitating and nourishing the relationship between people at many levels in *your* company with people at many levels in the *customer's* company. Most of the one-on-one wisdom of Carnegie still pertains. You simply need to apply this wisdom in ways that Carnegie never envisioned.

It's Not *Who* You Know, It's *What* You Know If the only weapons in your sales arsenal are your winning personality and your personal connections, your chances of achieving major success in today's competitive market are limited. That's because the typical buyer today—whether it's the customer in a retail store or the director of purchasing for a large corporation—is far more knowledgeable, more sophisticated, and more demanding than ever before.

Purchasing itself, especially on the corporate level, is more systematic and scientific than ever before, and buying decisions have become increasingly influenced by computer analysis. Shmoozing, in short, doesn't pay off the way it used to.

What does it all mean? Simply this: It is no longer *who* you know that gives you the competitive edge in selling; it is *what* you know—and how effectively you are able to use that knowledge to uncover and meet the needs of your customers.

3

PROFESSIONALISM
A Matter of Attitude

WHENEVER I INTERVIEW CANDIDATES for sales jobs these days, the one thing I look for more than anything else is attitude. I am interested in hiring only people who view themselves as *professionals*.

My favorite definition of professionalism comes from Harry Levinson, the author of *The Exceptional Executive*. In Levinson's view, a professional is someone who understands and is able to apply scientific knowledge to his or her work. It is someone who, because of this knowledge, can choose appropriate courses of action and is in charge of himself and his work.

Professionalism in sales is rooted in a vigorous respect for the sales process itself. It is viewing selling not simply as a "trade" or an "occupation," but in the same way that some military strategists define war: as an "art served by many sciences."

Selling can be legitimately described as an art because, like any art form, it calls for skills that you can enhance through practice. Serving this art is a science—a vast and growing body of knowledge covering the various aspects of the selling process, ready to be tapped by anyone committed to studying and mastering this body of knowledge.

I have never met a highly successful salesperson who did not approach every aspect of sales in a thoroughly professional manner. I have met hundreds of otherwise intelligent and talented people whose failure to achieve their potential in sales can be traced to one factor, above all: They didn't have enough respect for the process. They view sales not as a career, but as a stepping stone to something else.

I do not believe that you can succeed in a major way in sales with anything short of a professional attitude. That's because the attitude you bring to selling will have a profound influence on everything you do. It will influence how much time and effort you devote to learning about the products and services you sell, and how much interest you show in the needs of your prospects and customers. It will reflect itself in the attention you pay to detail, in how you organize yourself, in the way you dress and talk to people, and in the way you prepare for, conduct, and follow up on presentations.

Most important, though, the professionalism you bring to selling will go a long way to determine the quality of the relationships you establish with your prospects and customers—the trust you are able to inspire, and the loyalty you maintain. Because you yourself respect and take pride in what you do, the people you interact with on a day-to-day basis will treat you with more respect. Your day-to-day activities become more challenging and more meaningful. You savor your victories. You bounce back quickly from defeats.

Professionalism, in short, is the foundation of your success. It isn't a technique or something you turn on and off, like a light switch. It's a way of thinking, a way of life. You don't practice it—you live it.

4

CLOSING THE SALE
Updating an Old Paradigm

IN THE OLD-FASHIONED (some people refer to it as "old paradigm") approach to selling, most of what went on in a sales situation was nothing more than a prologue to the "close"—that critical moment when, by saying the right thing at the right time, you got the customer to "bite" and you "made" the sale. What happened after the "close"—how satisfied the customer was, for instance—was somebody else's problem, frequently the customer's.

A classic example of old-style, old-paradigm selling is the long-gone food freezer plan. You might remember it. The basic idea was to sell you a freezer. The gimmick was to throw in a large supply of frozen food at a substantial discount. As part of their training, the salespeople who went from door-to-door to sell the freezers were warned that if they gave customers time to think over the purchase, they would lose the sale. Why? Because it made no sense at all to buy an expensive appliance simply so you could save on the purchase of food.

So the ultimate—and only—purpose of the sales call was to "close": to manipulate the customer into saying *yes*.

A certain amount of this old-paradigm-type selling—sell it today and run for the hills—still goes on today. But among professionals selling quality products and services to major customers, the paradigm no longer works, not in an economy that has become so much more competitive and service oriented, and not in this era of heightened consumer awareness.

You are far better off in today's selling environment to think of "closing" not so much as a specific moment in a sale but, rather, as the entire selling process. The emphasis in selling has switched from "getting the customer to buy today" to "making sure the customer is happy tomorrow." You no longer manipulate the prospect into buying what you are selling. You focus on customer needs, and you fill those needs.

Ironically, the one place where this change has become especially visible is in what has historically been one of the bastions of old-paradigm, "close-the-sale" selling: your local car dealership. Yes, you still find remnants of the smooth-as-silk, "come on out and kick the tires" car salesman. What most successful dealerships sell today, though, is not only a new car but a service-based relationship with the customer.

I have a friend who bought a new Infiniti three months ago, and he tells me he has been called by a manufacturer's representative on four different occasions to make sure he's pleased with the purchase. This is not to mention the free loaner car or the complimentary car wash he gets whenever he takes the car in for service.

This changing perception of "closing" is particularly evident among major corporate buyers, most of whom are consolidating their purchasing practices, looking to establish long-term business relationships with fewer and fewer suppliers.

Consider the Ford Motor Company. At one time, Ford had more than six thousand suppliers. That number will eventually be reduced to less than a thousand. That means a lot of salespeople have lost a big customer, even though they might have had a great personal relationship with the buyer. The suppliers who have kept Ford as a customer have done so because they have developed an entirely new, service-oriented expertise—one that has enabled them to mobilize their corporate resources to give Ford the service it demands.

Consider, too, what has happened over the past five years with Procter & Gamble and its biggest customer, Wal-Mart. Five years ago, P & G had about twenty salespeople representing different departments traveling to Bentonville, Arkansas, to call on Wal-Mart. At Wal-Mart's request, Procter & Gamble's basic sales approach to this one customer has changed radically, with the objective being better service. More of the Procter & Gamble people who service Wal-Mart today live near the Bentonville headquarters. Most have job titles that designate them as logistical or service personnel—not salespeople.

The Wal-Marts and Fords of the world represent the future in purchasing. They don't want to be "sold." They want to be *served*.

Salespeople who understand and adapt to this change will prevail; those who don't will be left behind.

PART II

A FRESH LOOK AT SOME SELLING FUNDAMENTALS

☆

5

COURTESY
It Still Matters

DESPITE THE CHANGES THAT HAVE TAKEN PLACE in business over the past sixty years, and despite the new challenges you face today as a sales professional, one principle remains as important as it has ever been. It's called common courtesy.

Courtesy is so basic a consideration in selling that many sales trainers ignore it, figuring that most people are already familiar with the basics of common courtesy. I've discovered otherwise and have always made it a point whenever I work with new salespeople to emphasize the following points.

1 Be on Time Always. No excuses. There are enough elements of selling that are beyond your control. Don't take liberty with those elements that you *can* control.

2 Dress Appropriately The definition of *appropriate*, when you apply it to dress, varies according to where you live and what you sell. But if you are going to err, do it on the side of conservatism. Good grooming, of course, is essential in *every* instance.

3 Watch Where You Park Never park in parking spaces that might be otherwise used by customers.

4 Avoid Agenda Confusion Never allow your own deadlines or pressures to affect the attitude you convey to your customers. Don't make *your* agenda *their* agenda.

5 Don't Play Favorites Show everyone who works for your customers the same courtesy, regardless of how much or how little authority they have. A low-level employee today could become a key buyer tomorrow.

6 Lip Service Never smoke in a nonsmoker's office— even if you have been invited to do so.

7 When the Phone Rings If you are with a customer who has to take a phone call, excuse yourself. Doing so shows respect for the customer's privacy. It also avoids the embarrassment of being asked to leave.

8 Play It Safe Regardless of how well you think you know a customer, keep your business discussions free of anything that might be even remotely objection-able—particularly comments relating to sex, religion, race, or politics. Avoid foul language. Forget the dirty stories. Period. Period. Period.

9 Don't Knock Your Competitors Talking about your competitors is usually a no-win proposition. You don't help yourself by saying anything good about them, and dragging them through the mud can easily backfire. Whenever I am asked, "Who is your competition?" my standard response is to smile and say, "We don't have any."

10 Shake Hands Firmly and Look the Customer in the Eye It worked in Carnegie's time. It still works.

6

ON STAYING ORGANIZED
What Works for Me

I HAVE ALWAYS CONSIDERED MYSELF a reasonably well-organized person. But the older I get and the more cases I see of how the smallest of glitches can sabotage the largest of sales, the more organized I have become. Let me describe my own system.

First of all, I go everywhere with a portable computer and I use it for just about everything. But because the computer is not always convenient to use, I log my list of daily phone calls and related messages in a hard-cover notebook. I also include in this notebook any notes from conversations I have with customers. The benefit: I have only one place to look for a record or reminder.

The notebook I use is less than one-half-inch thick and has about one hundred fifty blank pages. You can find it among the ledger books in any good stationery store. One notebook normally lasts me about a year. When it's filled, it becomes part of my business reference library. I periodically photocopy my notebook, along with my address book. If I lose them, I have a backup. A note on the front page of the book gives my name and address and offers a one-hundred-dollar reward for its return.

My briefcase has several pockets, and every pocket always contains the same items. I can check the contents easily, and seldom forget to bring something I need on a sales call.

For a large presentation, I keep a checklist of everything I need to review before I enter the meeting room. It includes reminders for the following:

Know vital information about key participants

Check the location of light switches before I begin the presentation

Test the overhead projector and make sure I have a spare bulb for it

Locate the temperature control and make sure I know how it works

Have pens and notepad handy

Have blank transparencies

Check the line of sight from the fringe seats

Do a final check of the visuals

You may think that by double-checking all of these things before I begin my presentation, I am putting added pressure on myself. The opposite is true. Being systematic and organized relaxes me. It frees me from that all-too-common anxiety that comes from worrying that something you didn't think about might go wrong.

I read once that tennis champion Chris Evert got into the habit early in her career of packing her tennis bag in exactly the same way every time, putting each article of clothing in the same place. Asked why she was so methodical about such a seemingly unimportant thing, she replied, "When I'm in the locker room getting ready for a match, I don't want to think about anything except the match."

No one system works for everyone. The impor-

tant thing, though, is to have a system—and to stick
to it.

7

THE MOST IMPORTANT WORD IN A SALESPERSON'S VOCABULARY

I WAS HAVING LUNCH RECENTLY with several of my col-
leagues, all of whom are successful sales professionals, and the discussion at one point focused on what
each of us considered the most important attribute
you could have as a salesperson. It isn't very often
you get professional salespeople to agree on *anything,*
but in this case, we were all of a single mind. We all
agreed that the one quality above all others you must
bring to sales today is the ability to inspire trust.

What has always fascinated me about trust and
the role it plays in sales is how keenly aware of it we
are when we are the buyers, and how easy it is to lose
sight of when we are the sellers. A few Saturdays
ago, for example, I went with my wife to buy a new
set of tires for her car. On the road we drove along
as we headed to our tire dealer, there were three tire
stores, each offering the same brand of tires we were
looking for, and in at least one case, offering it a
lower price.

Even so, we kept driving until we came to the

tire dealer we'd been buying from for the past ten years. We knew from having dealt with this dealer for so long that if we didn't really need tires, he would tell us so. He had won our trust and, in the process, our loyalty.

Notice I said *won* our trust. That's an important consideration. Trust isn't something you inherit or automatically gain simply because you look and act like a trustworthy person. Trust is something you earn over time—not through your words but through your actions. And even when you have earned the trust of a customer, you can never take it for granted. You can lose trust in a moment of thoughtlessness. Once it's lost, trust is all but impossible to recover. You need to think of trust as though it were an incredibly beautiful but extremely fragile vase.

There are no secrets to building trust. It starts with making the welfare of your customers your main priority—even when it doesn't bring you personal gain. You never promise what you can't deliver, and you break your neck to deliver whatever you promise. Always.

8

THE SELLING PROCESS
The McDonald's Lesson

EVERY SALE, REGARDLESS OF WHAT IS BEING SOLD, how it is sold, and how much money is involved, is invariably the product of a process—a systematic sequence of events. The process takes place whether you're aware of it or not. The question is if you understand the process—and, more important, whether or not you are able to exercise reasonable control over each component in the process.

Consider one of the most familiar sales processes in the world. It is what happens when you go to McDonald's.

It starts when you are greeted ("Good afternoon . . ."), and are asked to give your order ("May I take your order?").

After you have given your order, it is repeated back to you (a simple but effective way of avoiding mistakes). You are then usually asked if there is something else you would like ("Would you like an order of french fries with that?"). The order is assembled and presented. You pay the bill, you are thanked, and you are asked to come again.

A simple process, yes, but it covers most of the bases in selling, and it sure does work.

When was the last time you stopped to think about the process that produces the sale in *your* business? Do you understand it? Have you instituted steps that give you control over it?

Here's a quick exercise to do either on your own, or with your sales team. Go through the steps that produce a typical sale: Think about how you generate leads and how you convert leads to contacts; talk about your selling argument and whether you have any way of knowing if your message is getting across.

See if you can outline the process, or put it on a flowchart.

Analyze the process. Is it logical? Does it do everything the McDonald's process does? Is there a step that reduces errors and encourages more sales? Is it easy to implement?

To repeat what I said earlier, your current sales approach already represents a process. The question is whether that process is a genuine blueprint for success. If it isn't, go back to the drawing board.

IF YOU CAN'T BE A GORILLA, BE A GUERRILLA

O ONE OF THE GREAT PASSIONS IN MY LIFE is reading about military history, and one of the specialties I have developed as a result of this interest is writing and lecturing about the parallels between successful military strategy and successful selling strategy.

There are many such parallels (some of which I will be mentioning throughout this book), but one observation from Carl von Clausewitz, the German military strategist, has always remained foremost in my mind—primarily because it relates to a selling principle that many salespeople fail to appreciate and exploit. The observation goes like this:

Where absolute superiority is not attainable, you must produce a relative one at the decisive point by making skillful use of what you have.

To paraphrase Clausewitz, you have to direct your strengths—whatever those strengths may be—to where they are likely to produce the best results. To express the idea in another way: "When you can't be a gorilla, be a guerrilla."

The main difference between a gorilla and guerrilla is that a gorilla fights *with* overwhelming strength whereas a guerrilla fights *against* overwhelming strength. Gorillas win by being, well, gorillas. They stake out whatever territory they want to occupy in the business jungle and they try to dominate it.

Guerrillas, on the other hand, win by following Clausewitz's advice. They never to try to beat gorillas by playing by the gorilla's rules. They look for openings where they can achieve relative superiority. They win by going into places where gorillas haven't—or can't—go, by doing things gorillas can't do.

On occasion in my career, I have been in a gorilla position, and it certainly has its advantages. When you're selling a product that is well known and widely accepted, your customers are frequently presold. Just ask Joe Peca, a successful sales entrepreneur who sells Amway and reports that many of the prospects he approaches are ready to sign up even before he's made his presentation. That's the power of the Amway name.

More often than not, however, I have had to operate—as do most people in sales today—as a sales guerrilla. This means I have be aware at all times of how the strengths of the product or service I am selling match up against the strengths of the gorillas who were my competition. I have learned through painful experience that, as a guerrilla, you never win a head-to-head battle with a gorilla. What I do instead is stress those aspects of my product or service that gorillas can't match.

The gorilla/guerrilla principle applies to all aspects of the selling process, including promotion and publicity. The company I now work for, Tennessee Associates, doesn't have the gorillalike resources to advertise on a major scale or to engage the services of a public relations agency. Even so, we manage to generate visibility.

I get publicity for myself and my company by writing articles. Other executives in our company are active in organizations and are frequently invited to speak at conferences. Our experience has been that whenever we get any sort of publicity—whether it is through an article or a conference—it usually produces a number of good, solid leads.

We compete very well against gorillas because we know our strengths, and we make the most of our skills.

10

WHAT YOU CAN LEARN FROM YOUR COMPETITORS
Advice from Sun-tzu

"KNOW YOUR ENEMY AND KNOW YOURSELF; and in a hundred battles you will never be defeated."

So wrote the Chinese military strategist Sun-tzu nearly twenty-five hundred years ago. Like so much that has been written about military strategy, it has direct application to successful selling in the 1990s.

Few of us have the luxury of selling to a captive

audience. As good as we are and as attentive as we are to our customers, there are others out there who want the business as badly as we do and who might be working just as hard to get it. Ignoring the competition can be a fatal mistake.

Getting to know your competition involves more than having a working knowledge of their products and their marketing and merchandising techniques. Your real goal is to learn the character and personality of your competitors. Once you learn how your competitors think, you can usually predict and anticipate what they're going to do.

There are any number of ways to find out what your competition is up to. Most are pretty basic. You should keep, and constantly update, a file of your competitors' product brochures, advertisements, and newsletters. Read trade magazines and clip all articles about competitor activity.

One of the ways I have always kept track of what my competitors are doing is attending trade shows and striking up conversations with anyone I can find (a supplier, for instance) who is familiar with my competitors. What I am looking for in these conversations is any information that can give me a competitive edge.

The most valuable information in this regard is anything that might suggest a weakness—some feature that customers are not happy with. Whenever I uncover this information, I file it away in the back of my mind and wait for the right place and time to mention it. I never mention that weakness directly. What I do instead is steer my sales presentation to that particular area of competitor vulnerability and stress the strength of my own product. I will say something like, "What you'll like about our product is . . ." or "The most useful aspect of our service is . . ." and introduce the strength that stands in contrast to my competitor's weakness.

One final point on learning about the competition: Don't limit your efforts to your *direct* competitors. I consider as competition *anyone* who is selling to my customers, regardless of the product or serving being sold. Why? Because anything my indirect competitors are selling to my customers could reduce the money the customers will be able to spend with me, in which case, these "indirect" competitors suddenly become direct competitors.

It is also possible, though, that what other people are selling to my customers could *increase* my business. If one of the products I'm selling is something that might be used on a boat, and another company has begun to sell boats to my customer, I want to share in that new business. I might want to form an alliance with the boat company—not only because it will increase the business I do with my current customer, but because it could also bring me business with that boat company's other customers.

11

WHERE THERE ARE PEOPLE, THERE IS OPPORTUNITY

Most successful salespeople I know have optimistic natures. The glass is never half empty, it's half full.

I'm thinking now of Stony Whitaker from Bell Buckle, Tennessee. Stony was the star shoe salesman of the year in a territory from which his predecessor had quit in disgust, sending back the message: "There's no potential here. Everyone goes barefoot." After a few months in the new territory, Stony proclaimed: "There's tremendous potential here. Everyone goes barefoot."

At the next national sales meeting, Stony was asked to deliver a presentation on his success. When he stepped up to the podium, he saw all the people in front of him and he got stage fright. All he could mumble into the microphone was his terrified reaction to the audience. "See the people," he mumbled. "See the people." He then sat down.

There was a moment of stunned silence. Then, suddenly, the hall burst into thunderous applause. Everyone in the room chose to see in those few simple words the essence of Stony's success: "See the people, and you will see opportunity."

12

KEEP YOUR SUNNY SIDE UP

Positive attitudes are self-perpetuating. Just ask successful athletes like Michael Jordan or Joe Montana. If you feel like you're on a roll, you *are* on a roll. The good things that happen are a *symptom* of the positive attitude and not the cause.

Regrettably, negative attitudes are also self-perpetuating. They lead ultimately to the classic bad sales line, "You wouldn't want to buy this vacuum cleaner, would you?" Everything else being equal, people are more likely to buy an inferior product from an upbeat salesperson than a superior product from someone who seems negative, down, listless, and uninterested.

Selling success thrives on being positive. It isn't always easy, of course, to maintain a positive attitude—especially when you're not getting the results you want. Like everyone in sales, I've had my share of peaks and valleys. Through the years, though, I have developed some techniques for getting myself out of those valleys. Here is some advice, based on a few things that work for me.

1 Remember the Good Times When things are tough, I think back to my most recent positive selling experience and I try to relive that experience mentally. The key to this technique is to take your time and envision as vividly as possible everything that went on during that previous experience: who the people were; what they said; how you reacted; how you felt when the sale came through. Act as if you had video-taped the experience and were watching it in its entirety.

2 Live for the Selling Moment If you find yourself feeling down just before going into a sales presenta-tion, take a moment beforehand to pump yourself up mentally. Imagine that you have an air pump. Go through the process of pumping air into your shoes. Feel the exhilaration surging through your body.

3 Hang Out with Winners Enthusiasm is conta-gious—so one of the best ways to keep yourself pumped up and primed for success is to spend time with people who are also pumped up and primed for success. Seek out people or situations (a gym rather than a bar, for instance) that you know will provide positive reinforcement. Avoid people who are downers.

4 Get a Couple of Wins Under Your Belt Whenever I have a new product or program to sell, I try to make my first call on a friendly account, where I can pretty much count on a sale. Doing so not only gives me a chance to practice my presentation, it also gives me a chance to taste success before I tackle bigger ac-counts. It puts me into a winning groove.

5 Don't Worry About "Losing" If you sell every pros-pect, you aren't making enough calls. If everything you try is a sure thing, you aren't taking enough risks. If you never fail, you put a limit on the degree to which you can succeed. In short, the only way to win big in selling is to risk losing.

To assume this risk, you must be able to handle rejection. You must be able to view rejection not as a defeat but as an opportunity to learn more about yourself and what you must do to succeed.

I have learned more from my sales failures than from my successes—particularly when I've looked back and asked myself why I lost the sale. More important, I have learned to accept rejection as part of the job. It comes with the territory.

I have a simple system that could work for you. Whenever I am selling—and particularly whenever I am prospecting—I keep a list in my mind of my top ten "sure things"—that is, the prospects on my list that I feel are the most likely to become customers.

I am aware, of course, that in selling there is no such thing as a "sure thing," but I play the game anyway. In the event one of my "sure things" doesn't pan out, I don't panic. I simply look for another prospect to add to the list.

What this simple little mind game does for me— and what it can do for you—is keep my morale high. With so many "sure things," who can get discouraged?

13

BECOME AN EXPERT

A FEW WEEKS AGO, WHILE I was browsing in one of the new computer superstores, I saw an unusual sight. In one of the departments, there were four salespeople simply standing around with seemingly nothing to do. Nearby, though, were several customers waiting in a line to talk to one salesperson in particular, a woman who looked to be in her mid-twenties. When I asked one of the idle salespeople why everyone was waiting to talk to this one salesperson, he replied, "She's the expert."

Today, more than ever, you, as the sales professional, must function as the information lifeline to your prospects and customers. The more you can position yourself as an authoritative and reliable source of information, the more successful you are going to be. The proof of this principle is everywhere.

One of the main reasons Home Depot has become a leading business success story of the 1990s is that when you visit the paint department of the typical Home Depot, the person who waits on you knows paint products inside and out.

I learned recently about a young man who has become the number one sales rep in a New England-based company that sells and leases copy machines. He doesn't have a college degree and has never taken an advanced science course. Yet he can tell you everything you could possibly want to know about the technology and inner workings of every copy machine on the market. He can even explain to you the chemical process that controls the amount of toner that hits the page, and how this process differs from machine to machine.

How did he become such an expert? By spending a lot of time with company technicians, by reading, by asking questions, by watching machines being serviced.

Does this knowledge pay off? His record speaks

for itself: He sells twice as many copiers as any other
salesperson in the company.

You can never know *too* much about the products or services you sell, about the products and services your competitors sell, and about the customer
needs that these products and services are designed
to fill. Gaining this knowledge is a two-step process:
The first step is to make the commitment; the second step is to do whatever is necessary to follow
through on the commitment.

14

AIM HIGH

THERE IS A COMMON TRAP IN SELLING that is easy to fall
into and difficult to escape from once you're in it.
What happens is that you achieve modest success
with small accounts that are relatively easy to sell
and you lose the motivation to go after big accounts
that require more effort.

No one would ever say that selling big accounts
is *easy*. The competition is a lot tougher, and you
have to be willing to devote far more time to every
aspect of the sale than would be the case with smaller
accounts.

Still, the effort and the time are worth it. Apart
from the satisfaction that comes when you make a
big sale to a major account, there are three reasons
why big-account selling should figure strongly in the
sales goals you set for yourself each year.

1 Credibility Selling big companies gives you and your company more credibility. Big accounts become your "bell cows"—they lead the herd. The more big accounts you have, the easier it is to get others.

2 Self-protection Big companies in a competitive economy tend to gobble up smaller companies in mergers and acquisitions and are more likely than smaller companies to be around in ten years.

3 Leverage Big companies tend to move slowly. So the more difficult it is for you to work your way into a major account, the harder it is for your competitors to get you out. You can enhance your leverage by developing a broad range of support. Get to know everyone in the process flow. The more services you render, the more leverage you have.

15

GETTING BETTER (AND BETTER)

P EOPLE OFTEN ASK ME HOW I HAVE been able to maintain the enthusiasm I bring to my work each day, given the fact that I have been at it for so many years. "Don't you ever get bored with selling?" people want to know.

No, I don't get bored—and for a simple reason. For as long as I can remember, I have been driven by an impulse to get better and better, and I view my efforts to get better and better as a mountain whose peak I will never reach.

When I talk about "getting better," I am not talking about any one selling skill in particular but about every aspect of the selling process—everything from the psychology of selling in general to the often subtle differences in all the businesses I have to understand if I am going to serve my customers in the best way I know how.

Some people will tell you that they are too busy "selling" to spend time on their own self-development, but I have never accepted not having enough time as an excuse. You have to *make* the time. Can you name any accomplished professional performer—athlete, dancer, singer, actor—who doesn't spend a certain amount of hours every week (indeed every day!) getting better at his or her craft? I can't.

There are countless ways you can improve yourself. Here are some of the most common.

1 Read I have always been an avid reader, and I attribute much of the success I have enjoyed in my career to the fact that I have never lost my hunger for knowledge. Whenever I am on the road and have extra time, I visit the business department of a bookstore and look for titles that relate to what I do. I have read literally hundreds of books on selling. Yet, whenever I look through a book I have never read, I still manage to come up away with a new idea or a new wrinkle on an old idea.

I also believe strongly in self-help magazines, like *Success*, and I subscribe to newsletters like *Boardroom Reports* or *Bottom Line*. I clip articles that offer useful advice and I keep them in an active file.

2 Put Your Driving Time to Work Long before audio-tape players were common in cars, I gave portable tape players to all my salespeople, the idea being that they could listen to self-improvement tapes in their cars rather than tuning in to the "top forty."

Most cars today are equipped with built-in tape players. Moreover, the number of self-help audio programs available is mind-boggling.

You don't have to limit the tapes you buy to those sold in stores or advertised in direct-mail pieces. Whenever Robert Kahn, a busy retailing consultant, editor of a monthly newsletter, and member of the board at Wal-Mart hears about a conference he can't attend, he purchases the tapes of the conferences and listens to them while he drives.

I go one step further. I record my public presentations on sales and marketing, then listen to them on my way home and while en route to my other presentations. I do something else, too. I sometimes listen to a tape I made years ago and, in doing so, I rediscover techniques that worked for me at one time but for some reason, I had fallen out of the habit of using. I find that listening to tapes while traveling between calls is not only a good way to keep my knowledge up, it also keeps my attitude up.

3 Get Help Much of what I have learned in my life I have learned from other people—people I have sought out just for that purpose.

There is no reason you can't do the same, if you put your mind to it. Begin with your circle of friends. Select at least one who is not directly involved with your business but who can nonetheless be a sounding board for your ideas.

If you work for a large company, try to find a coach or mentor. More and more major companies now team inexperienced salespeople with seasoned

professionals, and I applaud the practice. It works—
provided there is a structured mechanism for giving
feedback.

I remember one sales call early in my career in
which the person who accompanied me on a sales
call mentioned that I had spent much of the sales
call pointing my pencil at the customer. I had always
known that pointing your finger at the customer was
a bad habit. But not until it was pointed out to me
did I realize that I was doing the same thing with my
pencil. I broke the habit immediately.

4 **Be Willing to Learn from Your Mistakes** I have always viewed life as a series of repeated scenes, and
have found this principle to be particularly relevant
to becoming better at sales. Over and over, in life
and in sales, we are presented with the same or similar sets of circumstances. Sometimes we prevail;
sometimes we don't. The more willing we are to
view ourselves objectively, the easier it is to learn
from our experiences. We learn to repeat the scripts
that produced successful experiences. We learn to
rewrite the scripts that produced unsuccessful experiences.

5 **Make the Extra Effort** The difference between first
and last place in the Olympics is often measured in
milliseconds. It is no different in selling. The difference between winning and losing the customer is
often only a few percentage points of effort.

Winners make the extra effort in training and in
every competitive event. Here are some of the extras
that can make an important difference.

Extra Calls Always aim high. The effort it takes to
make one extra customer contact each day adds up

to about twenty new contacts a month and more than two hundred and fifty a year.

Extra Selling Effort Always try to do something to ignite the sales process with every customer. If you can't walk away from a sales call with a big order, walk away with a small order. It is always easier to sell something to somebody who has bought from you before—regardless of the size of the order.

Extra Knowledge If you are not constantly studying your profession, your products, or your industry, you cannot improve.

Added Value Always look for ways in which you can imbue your product or service with a measure of added value that gives you an edge over your competition. Be proactive. Do things for customers before they ask. That way, you win in two ways: Your customers are appreciative and impressed with your ability to anticipate their needs.

PART III

BUILDING BUSINESS

The Art of Generating Leads and Corralling Prospects

☆

16

KEEP FEEDING THE FUNNEL

N O MATTER HOW WELL YOU ARE DOING with your current group of customers, you can never rest easy in sales unless you are constantly developing new customers. This means two things: one, generating leads; two, converting those leads into prospects.

To put this principle to practical use, I have found it helpful to work with a familiar symbol in sales training: a funnel. I know that if I want to have a steady stream of customers at the bottom of the funnel, I have to devote a certain percentage of my time feeding the top of the funnel.

I use an actual drawing of a funnel in my planning.

At the top of the funnel, I write down the various sources I rely on to feed the funnel—that is, the sources from which I generate leads. I include in this category activities like speaking at meetings and conferences, phone canvassing, advertising, referrals, personal networking, and so on. Whenever I uncover a lead through any of these activities, the name goes into the funnel.

To keep track of how well my lead sources are working, I write down the date each name enters the funnel. I review the funnel periodically, and if I see that the most recent date of acquisition in any group is over three months old, I know that area needs attention.

The funnel idea lends particularly well to phone prospecting. A common variation of funnel thinking is sometimes referred to as the "10-8-4-2-1." It works like this:

Call ten people on the phone, and eight will be at home. Four or them will say they can't talk to you, but the other four will engage you in conversation. Of those four, two will be interested in your product or service, and one will actually buy. What does this mean? If you want to make ten sales, you need to make one hundred phone calls.

The actual numbers that apply to a "funnel" in any given situation will vary according to any number of factors. In some industries, it takes 125 contacts to get five solid prospects, one of which will result in a sale. The principle, though, never varies.

One of the best—and most underutilized—ways of keeping activity high in the input side of the sales funnel is to become part of a network of professionals who share leads. If you are not part of such a group already, create one. This circle of professionals with mutual interests can be a rich source of business. Be sure to include noncompeting people from your industry. For example, a life insurance salesperson could invite auto and property insurance people.

When you begin to set up your funnel; it will help to separate it into five sections, based on the status of any contact:

Lead The name of a person or company that might represent a customer.
Suspect A person whom you have actually talked to but who has yet to express any interest in your product or service.

Prospect Someone with whom you are discussing a purchase.

Customer Someone who has recently made a purchase or buys regularly.

Previous Customer Someone who has previously purchased from you but hasn't been an active customer for a long time.

At any given time, each portion of your funnel should be filled with names of people and companies who fit into one of these categories. And remember, the key to making this principle work is to keep feeding the top. Otherwise, the bottom will dry up.

17

INITIATE NEW BUSINESS FROM THE TOP DOWN

WHENEVER I APPROACH A NEW PROSPECT, I never think twice about where I try to establish contact. I always start as high as I can. I have learned through experience that when my link to the buyer comes through a senior manager, it vastly increases my chances of making the sale.

You might have the impression, as many people do, that middle-level buyers resent it when you approach senior management before you come to them. That is a myth. What middle-level buyers resent is when you *start* with them, and then, if you don't make the sale, try to go higher. This tactic, by the way, can occasionally produce a sale. Generally, though, going over the head of someone who has buying authority is the kiss of death.

Selling from the bottom up is a long climb. Selling from the top down gets you where you want to be much quicker.

18

MAKING THE PHONE YOUR ALLY

USED PROPERLY, THE TELEPHONE CAN BE A TIME-SAVING ALLY. Ignore the few simple rules that follow, and the phone will turn into a costly obstacle.

1 Avoid Phone Tag If you don't know the person you're calling, never leave a message to call you back. Think about it. Why would anyone be eager to return a call to an unknown person who wants to sell an unsolicited product or service? Leaving such a message drastically reduces the possibility of a sale—even if your call *is* returned.

There are other reasons for not leaving a call-back message when you're calling someone you don't know. What happens if your call is returned and you are not available? The prospect now becomes even more irritated. If the call is returned days later, when you are mentally unprepared for it, you may even have forgotten your reason for calling. Having to ask people you are trying to sell who they are and what company they're with is insulting to the caller, and hardly the best way to begin a selling relationship.

2 Keep on the Offensive If the prospect is not available, try to find out when the person is likely to be in. Make suggestions: Later in the day? In two days? Be persistent, but don't push too hard.

3 Make Friends Keep in mind that the person answering the phone may be a business associate or a secretary of the prospect. Make that person your friend. Give your name freely. Get theirs. Write it down. Strike up a relationship.

4 Call at the Right Time Busy executives come in early and leave late. So the best time to get in touch with hard-to-reach prospects is just before or just after normal office hours, when secretaries are not around and managers tend to answer their own phones. Another good time to call is between noon and one o'clock, when the secretary is out to lunch.

5 Ask Permission You never know when you call someone how busy the person is and how receptive he or she is likely to be to your call. So don't launch into a lengthy conversation without first asking a question such as, "Do you have a moment?" Doing so saves you the embarrassment of being cut off in mid-sentence and being told to call back.

6 Listen Listen carefully to see if you can sense the mental state of the person you are calling. If the person seems rushed or agitated, offer to call back at a better time. And by all means, make sure *your* mood is friendly and engaging.

7 Learn How to Be Persistent Without Pestering

One of my favorite salespeople is fond of saying, "I keep in touch with my customers until they buy or die." That's good advice, but with one caveat: that you understand the difference between pestering and persistence.

Pestering is coming back to the same customer time and again, but with the same reason for buying. *Persistence* is keeping in touch, but using different techniques and different approaches to support your case.

Persistence is obviously harder to pull off: It obliges you to come up with new ideas—a new benefit, different payment terms, etc.—that will give the prospect a new reason for thinking about your product or service.

Prospects appreciate persistence. They let you know in not so subtle ways when persistence turns into pestering.

19

HOT IDEAS FOR COLD CALLING

D IVING INTO COLD-CALL PROSPECTING is a lot like diving into a cold swimming pool: It's tough to work up the courage to dive in when you're standing on the side of the pool. But once you're in the water, it's not so bad.

As in so many other aspects of selling, the attitude you bring to cold calling goes a long way toward influencing the results you achieve. Above all, you need to recognize that regardless of what you're selling, the odds in cold calling always work against you. Simply being able to connect with the right person is a victory in cold calling. If you can walk away from a cold-calling session having uncovered a single lead— just one!—you can consider yourself fortunate.

One of the things that helps me greatly whenever I do cold calling to get prospects is to keep in mind what I want to achieve. My objective in a cold call is not to sell my product or service. It is to get acquainted with the lead and to sell myself. So the main thing I think about before the call and throughout the call is to be as friendly and engaging as I can be.

Here are some additional suggestions about cold calling that should help you get better results.

1 Set Up the Right Atmosphere Cold calling needs a supportive atmosphere. That's why companies that do most of their business via cold-call selling hold daily pep meetings, and why the successful companies do their best to create a pleasant environment for their callers.

You can set up your own "pep atmosphere"— even if you work alone. It's mainly a matter of self-psyching. You prepare for your cold-calling session the way professional athletes prepare for important games. You set aside a block of time. You organize your working space. You make sure you feel well rested, and you do whatever you need to do to get yourself into a positive frame of mind.

2 Try to Make It a Lukewarm Call The best way to take the chill out of a cold call is to get a referral. Being able to use a name familiar to the person you want to talk to will almost always get you past the first stage of a cold call, so whatever time and effort are involved in getting that name is usually worth it. Your best source of names are your most satisfied customers.

3 Give Yourself Something to Talk About Sending something in advance—a letter or postcard introducing yourself—is yet another good way to break the ice on a cold call. It gives you a good opening line: "Last week, I sent you a letter on . . ." And here's a good idea to try if you get prospects' names out of newspapers or magazines: Send them a mounted reprint of the piece.

20

DO SOMETHING BIG AND UNUSUAL FOR BIG PROSPECTS

ONCE, WHEN I HAD A PROSPECT who was tough to reach, I had a messenger service deliver a sixty-six-inch-high stuffed Pink Panther to his office with a tag reading: "You'll be tickled pink with the opportunity I have for you—Jerry Michaelson."

When I called a few days later and identified myself as the guy who sent the Pink Panther, I got right through. Since then, I've sent out dozens of oversized Pink Panthers. As proof that the technique works, I recently received a phone call concerning new business from a previous client who had received a Pink Panther from me—over ten years ago.

I recall another occasion in which a prospect I had reached through cold calling insisted that before she would agree to an appointment, she wanted to see a brochure. I sent the brochure, but when I called back a week later, the woman insisted she hadn't received it. It was obvious to me that the woman was stalling, but I really wanted to sell this prospect. So, instead of sending another brochure by itself, I put it in a box that also contained a chocolate chip cookie the size of a pizza.

I knew I had done the right thing when I called back and heard the woman say, "That cookie made my day." The result was an appointment—and an order.

21

TRADE-SHOW INTELLIGENCE
The Power of Creative Disruption

TRADE SHOWS ARE AN EXCELLENT and often cost-effective way to gain visibility for your product or service, and to feed the prospect portion of your funnel. But unless you can attract people to your booth in significant numbers, the time and money that goes into setting up a display booth at a trade show is a waste of time.

The principle I have always followed whenever I have been involved with a trade-show booth is something I call *creative disruption*. Here is an example of what I mean.

I once wanted to send a message about the profit opportunity in video games to retailers attending a major industry trade show. What I did was to build a stack of money twenty feet high by eight feet wide in a glass case that towered up in the air. The stack contained a million dollars, bound in units of one thousand one-dollar bills.

The purpose behind this display was to make a point. The *strategy* behind the display was to be creatively disruptive and imaginatively intrusive.

I had determined that if a retailer could sell 1,786 video game master units a year, he would generate a demand for software that would eventually yield one million dollars in profit. I didn't expect retailers to believe that they could sell enough games to make a million dollars. I simply wanted to make a point. I think I did.

The typical reaction to the display was as follows: People would walk down the aisle, pass the display, glance to their right or left, and then— here's where the disruptive part comes in—do a double take. They would walk over to the throng and begin gazing at the money. Few people, I'm sure, had ever seen a million dollars in dollar bills, never mind a stack of bills twenty feet high.

Nearly everyone took the time to read about the million-dollar profit opportunity. Invariably, they would smile. As they walked away, an armed guard gave them a canvas money bag that had the product name on the outside, and brochures and a reply card on the inside. The disruptive and intrusive idea was reinforced in the copy that appeared on the coupon. It read:

"Yes, please send me more information. I'm interested in making a million dollars."

"No, I'm not interested in making a million dollars at this time."

The results were striking. In a typical trade-show promotion, we would distribute a few thousand brochures. For this event, we tripled the number of brochures. At that, we ran out of brochures on the second day of the four-day show.

Here's the best part. Within a few months, the dealer organization had doubled, and by the end of the year, business had increased three times over the previous year, with profits generating at an even higher multiple. The only really tough part of the promotion was getting the chief financial officer to agree to have a million dollars in one-dollar bills delivered to the trade show for a few days.

Keep the basic concept in mind. If you want someone to pay attention, first of all, you need to disrupt the mind, and then make a strategic intrusion into that disruption. The greater the disruption, the easier it is to intrude.

Of course, neither the disruption nor the intrusion can be crass or offensive. If the disruption simply shocks or puts people in a negative frame of mind, the strategy backfires. Finally, the intrusion must be directly related to the sales message you want to get across.

22

BUILD SUSPENSE

THE GREAT SALESMAN NOLAN BUSHNELL decided he wanted to expand from San Francisco into Oregon. He targeted a chain of retail stores in Oregon and sent the manager of each store a telegram. The telegram read, BUSHNELL IS COMING.

A few days later, as he worked his way up the coast, he sent a second telegram that read, BUSHNELL IS IN EUREKA. Every day, the store manager received another telegram advising them of the progress of the mysterious Bushnell. One day, they all received a large box marked, HOLD FOR BUSHNELL. Later, each of them received a telegram indicating the day and time of day when Bushnell would arrive in the flesh.

At the promised time, Bushnell arrived, asked for the carton, uncrated the product, made a demonstration, and made the sale.

How could anyone refuse such a highly focused and determined sales approach?

PART IV

CONVERTING PROSPECTS INTO CUSTOMERS

23

GETTING OFF ON THE RIGHT FOOT
How to Open the "Close"

AS I HAVE ALREADY EMPHASIZED, the "close," for all intents and purposes, is the *entire sales process*. It begins, in fact, with the impression you create when you meet or talk to a new customer for the first time. True, you can overcome a bad first impression, but the need to do so puts you under unnecessary pressure. Why risk it?

Here are some guidelines on how to get a selling relationship started on the right foot, based on my own experiences and on what I have learned from watching others.

1 Be Yourself One of the biggest mistakes you can make on your first call is to go out of your way to impress the customer with your own expertise or with the reputation of your company. Here's a secret that might surprise you. The one attribute that has more bearing than any other when it comes to establishing a solid sales relationship is sincerity. Ironically, the more you try to "impress" the customer, the harder it will be for you to make the personal connection that will be the basis of your relationship.

2 Establish Common Ground You can never have too much in common with the people to whom you sell.

The more commonality you can create, the more the customer will trust you and the easier it will be for you to gain the trust that is the cornerstone of a successful salesperson/customer relationship. Some suggestions follow:

- The first time you enter a customer's office, look at what is on the wall, on the desk, and on the shelves. If you're impressed, make a sincere comment of admiration. Otherwise, find an item of interest and ask about it.
- Without being too obvious about it, spend a moment or two before you get to the business side of your discussion to establish common areas of interest: kids, sports, mutual friends. A simple question like, "Did you watch the game (or a certain television show) last night?" can establish a link.
- Listen to the "beat" of the customer. That is, pay attention to the customer's state of mind at the time of your meeting. Is the customer up or down today? In a patient mood or in a hurry? Do your best to match your own pace with that of the customer.
- Refer to your prospect by name as often as possible, but without overdoing it. It helps to personalize the relationship.

3 Lighten Up for Group Presentations Establishing common ground with a group of people you have never met—something you often have to do when you are making a group presentation—is tough to do, but I have found humor to be an excellent icebreaker.

When I am selling my own company's services, for instance, I will often begin by asking, "Will everyone in favor of creating a high-performance organization raise his or her hand?" This somewhat absurd question usually earns a chuckle. More important, it gives me a lead-in to what I really want to talk about, which is the difference between *believing* in quality and high performance and implementing quality and high performance.

4 Take Notes Here are three good reasons for taking notes:

- *It helps you remember.* When it comes to making promises to a prospect or a customer, you can't afford to rely on your memory. Write everything down. After each meeting, check your notes and use them as the basis of an action plan.
- *It impresses the prospect.* When prospects see that you consider what they are saying sufficiently important to write down, they develop more confidence in you. Taking notes also helps protect your credibility if a misunderstanding develops or if someone else in the response chain drops the ball.
- *It helps organize your thinking.* Tom Monaghan, founder of Domino's Pizza, is known for taking voluminous notes on yellow pads. The reason he does this, he has explained, is not so much to help him remember what went on during the meeting but to help him think things through when the meeting is over. What Monaghan has learned is that seeing your ideas in writing helps crystallize your thoughts and propels you to come up with great ideas.

5 Be Mindful of Little Things Don't overlook these details:

- Get rid of your outer coat before you walk into a customer's office. (Walking into a customer's office with your coat on automatically makes you look as if you don't belong. If you are wearing a coat, hang it up in the reception area or leave it on a chair.)

- Try to arrange it so that you sit *alongside* the customer, rather than on the other side of the desk. Having a barrier between the two of you diminishes your persuasive power.

- Seek the same eye level as the customer. If the customer is standing, you should stand. If the customer is seated, you should sit.

- Make sure that when you walk out of the office, you never leave behind anything that needs to be cleaned up—like an empty cup.

- Make sure that in a group presentation, your own salespeople are interspersed among the customer's people. Having your group on one side and the customer's group on the other side reinforces the "us" versus "them" mind-set.

24

CONTROL THE FLOW

I AM PROBABLY A LITTLE MORE COMPULSIVE about how I organize and sequence my sales calls than most salespeople, but there's a good reason. Early in my career, I was competing with another salesperson for a big chunk of business with a major chain. My competitor ended up with the business, and the main reason, I found out from my contact at the account, is that his presentation had been much better organized and focused than mine.

The silver lining around this cloud is that I spoke at length with my contact about what my competitor had done during his presentation, and I eventually incorporated much of what I learned during that conversation into my own presentation techniques.

What follows is a broad outline of how to sequence a typical sales call. Naturally, you need to adapt this model to individual situations, and you have to keep in mind that any number of factors— time constraints, the number of people you're presenting to, the type of product or service you are selling—will dictate the way you actually use the model.

1 Breaking the Ice Some sales professionals refer to this stage of a sales call as the "small talk" part. What you are trying to do here is to establish rapport—to put your prospect or customer in a receptive frame of mind. The time you spend in this stage of a presentation will vary depending upon the situation (that is, how busy the customer is), the relationship you have with the prospect or customer, and the type of person you are dealing with. I always take my cues from the prospect. If I see he or she wants to keep the small talk going, I don't push things. If I sense that a customer wants to get to the business part of the discussion right away, I move forward.

2 Establishing Needs Once you get past the preliminaries, the focus of your presentation should shift to your prospects and their needs. During this stage of the presentation, you should be asking questions, listening, probing for more detailed answers, and listening even more.

3 Verifying Needs Verifying the prospect's needs is something I did not do enough of early in my career, and something that many salespeople fail to do. Your goal during this stage of the presentation should be to get the prospect's needs nailed down. The prospect may have communicated to you any number of needs, and it's important to get a sense of priorities. Which of the needs is the most pressing?

4 Presenting Solutions Depending upon what you are selling, your solutions to the needs you have uncovered during the previous two stages of your presentation will come either during this presentation or during another sales call. In either event, you need to be superattentive to the prospect's responses. You can usually tell, often by a person's body language or by the responses you get, if your solutions are pressing the right buttons or not. If you think your message is hitting the proverbial stone wall, you should be prepared to deviate from your original plan. One of the reasons I have never liked or advocated carefully scripted "presentations" is that they give you no margin for error in the event the prospect isn't receptive.

5 Handle Objections The main thing to keep in mind about handling objections is to welcome them. View them as requests for more information. Objections give you an opportunity to reemphasize your key selling points. I would much rather have objections come to the surface during the call, when I can address them, than to have prospects keep the objections to themselves.

6 Ask for the Order Sooner or later, you have to get the customer to commit. For more details, see page 91.

25

THE TROUBLE WITH "MAY I HELP YOU?"

I F I WERE SELLING PRODUCTS IN A RETAIL STORE, the last thing you would ever hear me say to a customer is the one thing retail salespeople say over and over: "May I help you?" The reason? "May I help you" violates one of the cardinal rules of successful selling. It is one of those questions that could conceivably produce the last word you want to hear whenever you are having a conversation with a prospect. That word is *No*.

How do you get around asking such a common question? Well, you can do what a salesman did not long ago when I was looking for some boots at a Nordstrom's in Anchorage, Alaska. Instead of saying, "May I help you?" the salesman, flashing a friendly smile, said, "If you find something you like, we probably have it in your size." What a great, positive comment.

I am reminded, too, of a super-successful automobile salesman I know who uses the same question over and over, regardless of whom he approaches. I have been with him at restaurants when he has said to the waiter or waitress, "If I could put you in a car you would like to own at a price you would like to pay, would you be interested?" You would be astonished at how many how positive answers he generates and how many sales that ultimately result from the question.

Get your prospects accustomed to saying *Yes*. Create *yes* situations at the beginning and throughout the presentation, and you stand a good chance of getting the yes answer that really counts.

26

PRESENTING YOUR CASE
Why Less Is More

I F I HAVE LEARNED ANYTHING IN MY CAREER about sales presentations, it is simply this: Less is almost always more. Short presentations that hammer home a few key points are invariably more persuasive than long, drawn-out presentations that attempt to cover every conceivable aspect of your product or service. People rarely remember the particulars of a presentation. What sticks in their mind—make that what *should* stick in their minds—are the two or three ideas that have direct relevance to their needs.

One simple technique that helps me immeasurably in the presentations I deliver is something I think of as the "magical three." Here are some tips that relate to this technique.

1. Never give your prospects more than three reasons for buying your product or service. The longer your list, the less likely the prospect will remember the most important selling points.
2. Never have more than three topics on any flip chart, flyer, or slide at one time. If a longer listing is necessary, break it into three subheadings, with three smaller points under each.
3. If your customers need to convey your information to someone else in the organization, give them only three things to remember: the three main reasons for buying from you.

27

SHUT UP AND LISTEN

Highly successful salespeople are often—and incorrectly—stereotyped as gifted talkers. The fact is that the most successful salespeople I know, good as they are at talking, are even better at an aspect of selling that is far more important than the ability to talk: the ability to listen.

There is no way that I can overemphasize the importance of being a good listener in any sales situation. The more attentively you listen, the easier it becomes for you to learn which buttons to push and which buttons to avoid. You learn what really matters to the prospect, and you are then in a better position to focus your efforts on those concerns that will increase your credibility and produce the sale.

I can't tell you how many times in my career I thought I knew what the prospect wanted, only to discover after my presentation that the two of us were on different wavelengths—that what I was selling was not what the prospect was buying. I had to learn the hard way that the only way to get a true fix on what a prospect needs is to *force* yourself to listen, to block out distractions, and to hold in check the tendency to think about your reaction to what the prospect is saying rather than what is actually being said.

Here are some simple guidelines that relate to being a good listener in a sales situation. As you read through them, try to think of them within the framework of your own listening habits.

1 Pay Attention to What Is Being Said Nearly all of us have the tendency I mentioned earlier. We pay too much attention to our *reaction* to what is being said (and how we want to respond), instead of putting the full measure of our attention on what is *actually* being said.

There's an easy way to tell if you are a victim of this tendency. Think about how often you find yourself constantly stepping on your prospect's last words, rushing in with answers right after the prospect has finished making a point.

I broke this self-defeating habit by training myself never to talk while the customer was talking. I find that I have plenty of time, once the customer has finished talking, to think about my response. This discovery, in turn, made me a much better, much more attentive, listener.

2 Paraphrase What You Think You Have Heard Whenever a prospect expresses a thought or opinion, get into the habit of reiterating in your own words what you've just heard. Doing so accomplishes two things: One, it reduces the likelihood of misunderstanding what was said; two, it massages the prospect's ego. People like to hear what they've just said repeated. It makes them feel important.

3 If You Don't Understand, Ask Never assume anything. If you don't know exactly what the customer means or wants, don't hesitate to ask.

4 Listen with Your Entire Body One of the little-known keys to better listening lies in the fact that you don't listen simply with your ears. You listen with your eyes and, for that matter, with your entire body. Become more sensitive to your body language as you are listening, and your listening habits will automatically improve.

Eye contact is especially important, but you have to remind yourself continually to do it. Posture is important, too. I know, for example, that when I am making a conscious effort to listen to what another person is saying, I invariably lean forward. If I find myself slouching or looking somewhere other than in the direction of the speaker, it's a sign that I have lost focus.

One more thing: Nearly everything I have just said about listening when you are face-to-face with a customer applies as well to what you should be doing when you are talking on the phone.

28

FOCUS ON BENEFITS

THERE ARE THREE WAYS YOU CAN TALK about your product or service during a sales call. You can focus on its features, its advantages, or its benefits. The easiest thing to do is to talk about features and advantages. The best thing to do is to focus on benefits.

Here are the differences:

A *feature* is any characteristic, specification, or attribute of your product or service: what the product or service *is* or *does*. If you are selling air conditioners, for instance, features would include things like its BTU rating, its energy efficiency, its size, and its temperature-control system.

An *advantage* is something your product has or does that a competitive product doesn't have, doesn't do, or doesn't do well. For example, the advantage an air conditioner you are trying to sell might enjoy over a competitor's is that it is quieter or uses less energy.

A *benefit* is a feature or advantage that means something to the prospect. It answers a need. The "benefit" implicit in the energy efficiency of an air conditioner is the money the customer saves each month when the utility bill arrives.

Focusing on the benefits of your product or service instead of the features or advantages is hardly a new idea in selling, but it is such an important concept in selling that it can never be overemphasized—particularly since some salespeople have problems differentiating advantages from true benefits.

Let's go back to the air conditioner example. If you were selling someone who was extremely concerned about monthly utility bills, the fact that a particular model air conditioner could keep the customer's monthly utility bills down would represent a true benefit.

Why? Because it meets an *explicit* need.

If, on the other hand, the customer didn't really care one way or the other about the extra fifteen or twenty dollars in monthly bills that a particular model might bring, the savings is no longer a benefit—not in this situation, at any rate. The chief benefit for *that* customer might be the fact that the air conditioner is extremely quiet. Or, to express the same idea in a benefit statement, "The air conditioner is so quiet, you will never know it's on."

The two key points to remember:

1. Always bear in mind the distinction between the features or advantages of the product or service you are selling and the tangible benefits those features or characteristics offer the prospect.
2. Make sure you build your presentation around true benefits—those benefits that meet the explicit needs of your prospects and customers.

29

SELL THE SOLUTION

IF YOU WERE TO CALL UP YOUR FAMILY DOCTOR and say, "I need some penicillin," your doctor's likely reply would be: "What's wrong with you? What are your symptoms?" Doctors are trained to treat symptoms and solve problems—not simply to prescribe medicine.

I think it's fair to say that the most successful people in sales view themselves in many ways as doctors do—as problem solvers. They know that the best way to generate sales is to get an accurate reading on what the customer needs, and to provide a product or service that fills that need. What enables successful salespeople to operate this way is their mental focus: what they concentrate on whenever they call on prospects or customers.

Here's a story that illustrates as well as any incident I've heard about the value of bringing to every sales situation a solution-oriented point of view.

A woman I know of, who heads a small communications consulting firm, was invited several months ago to make a presentation to a large manufacturing firm that wanted to produce a four-color brochure. The subject of the brochure was employee safety. The plan was to distribute the brochure to supervisors throughout the company in the hope that it would stimulate a greater degree of safety awareness.

As it happens, the woman was one of ten people invited to make a presentation. As she learned later, she was the only one of the ten who didn't come to the presentation armed to the teeth with sample brochures.

What she brought with her instead was a clipboard and a legal pad. And instead of spending the half-hour she had been allotted trying to prove to the group what an able writer and designer she was, she asked questions. Lots of them. What interested her mainly was whether the people interviewing her had a legitimate reason for believing that a brochure, regardless of how well it was done, would bring about the greater sense of safety awareness that they were trying to create.

They didn't. The fact is, once the idea for the brochure had been proposed, no one in the company had stopped to think about whether it represented a true solution to the problem the company was trying to solve.

The company never did create a brochure. Instead, it created a six-month program that combined a do-it-yourself audit, combined with a contest, and supported by three bi-monthly newsletters. The budget for the creative work and the printing stayed the same.

Who do you think got the job?

30

UNIQUE PROPOSITIONS
Selling and Buying

MARKETING CONSULTANTS OFTEN PREACH about the importance of identifying and using in your sales and marketing strategy the Unique Selling Proposition (USP) of your product or service—the one quality (or qualities) that sets your product or service apart from the competition and provides a true benefit to the customer.

I agree that USP is a powerful sales and marketing concept, but it takes on even more power when you combine it with something that might best be described as the Unique *Buying* Proposition—the one aspect of your product or service that is likely to have special appeal to your prospect.

No one I know puts the combination of USP and UBP to better use than Alice Rutten, a highly successful real estate broker whose specialty is selling houses nobody else can sell.

A few years ago, for instance, Alice was approached by a tile contractor who wanted to sell his house. Other real estate brokers had looked at the house and had decided that it wasn't very marketable. It had tile *everywhere*—not just in the kitchen and the bath but in every room in the house. In some rooms, even the ceilings were tiled.

Alice wasted no time in putting the USP/USB principle to work. The first thing she did after agreeing to sell the house was to call several tile contractors listed in the Yellow Pages. She knew that the only person who might be interested in this kind of house was somebody who appreciated tile. She was right. Even before she listed the house, she found a customer.

Here's another Alice USP/USB story. She was once faced with the challenge of selling a house that was located in an affluent suburb but also happened to be very close to the railroad tracks. The railroad tracks, in fact, were right in front of you when you entered the driveway.

Here again, as she had with the tiled house, Alice identified the USP of the house and converted it to a UBP. She ran an ad in the local newspaper with a headline that appealed to a unique interest. The headline read: DO YOU LIKE TRAINS? The house sold quickly—to a family who had always lived near railroad tracks and liked it. When Alice stopped by later to take the new owners out to dinner, their children told her that as a reward, when they were good, they were allowed to stay up to watch the nine o'clock train.

Matching USPs and UBPs is a selling technique that can work wonders for you in almost every industry. It's a particularly useful technique in any

business—retailing, for instance—in which you deal
with a great many products and a large number of
customers.

One of the most successful retailing salespersons
in New York is a woman who works for a leading
women's store. For the past fifteen years, she has
maintained a file of five- by eight-inch index cards.
Each card bears the name of a customer, along with
notes that describe the kinds of clothes (style, col-
ors, etc.) the woman likes. Whenever her store re-
ceives a shipment, she reviews the merchandise and
then goes to her files, looking for customers likely to
be interested in specific pieces. She has become so
proficient at knowing what her customers like that
she frequently makes big sales over the phone, simply on the basis of her recommendations.

31

SCOPE IT UP OR DOWN

SCOPING IS A VERSATILE AND OFTEN EFFECTIVE technique whose purpose is to amplify the appeal of
benefits and minimize the apparent downside of cost
and other negatives. You "scope up" to accentuate
the positives—like savings or value. You "scope
down" to minimize the negative—like investment,
time, or effort.

A simple way to "scope up" benefits is to take
the annual return and multiply it by the useful life of
the product or service. For example, $100,000.00

annual savings times ten years equals $1,000,000.00 savings. (Note the two extra zeros after the decimal point, which make the savings look even bigger.)

One of the best salespeople who ever worked for me liked to approach new prospects with this statement: "How would you like to make a million dollars?" He wasn't talking about the profit the account would make in a year. He was "scoping up" the profit that could be made in a lifetime. He would then proceed to validate his claim by proving the annual profit opportunity and multiplying that out to the maximum.

"Scoping down" involves the same principle, only in reverse. $100,000 in annual costs sounds like a lot of money—even without the decimal point and the two zeroes. Divided by 250 business days, however, it works out to $400 per week. Divided by five business days in a week, the cost goes down to $80 per day. Divided by an eight-hour day, the cost becomes only $10 per hour.

Burt Bemister, a salesperson who worked for me years ago, used "scoping down" over and over to sell advertising on a giant $15,000 outdoor sign. Instead of focusing on the price, he stressed that the sign would last for ten years and would therefore cost only $1,500 per year. He went further, pointing out that the per-diem cost of keeping the sign illuminated for 365 nights and clearly visible for 365 days was less than $2.

Burt sold more signs than anyone who worked for me. In the process, he helped customers sell more of the products advertised on the signs.

32

GET PERSONALITY-TYPE SMART

B EING ABLE TO ADAPT YOUR OWN SELLING STYLE to the
personalities of your customers can be an enormous advantage in your sales efforts, and there are
several programs and systems that purport to teach
you this skill. The only problem is that many of
these programs and systems, while interesting to go
through and to read about, are not as applicable to
day-to-day selling as one would hope.

A notable exception is the Meyers-Briggs Type
Indicator (MBTI), whose concepts I have found
both interesting *and* practical. This model, like similar ones, divides people into various personality categories, based on how they like to operate their lives
in general, how they like to gather information, and
how they like to make decisions. What makes the
Meyers-Briggs model different is that the categories
are more clearly defined than they are in other models, and therefore are easier to recognize and work
with.

Among other things, MBTI training teaches you
how to identify the category into which you yourself
fit, and how to identify the categories into which
your customers fit. You are then taught to make
adjustments in your own style so that you and the
person to whom you are trying to sell are operating
on the same wavelength.

Here is one small example of what MBTI training teaches, and how the training applies to sales.

One of the categories the MBTI model uses is decision-making style. The model divides people into two broad personality groups: thinkers and feelers.

Thinkers tend to base their decisions on logic. They are usually objective: they usually base their decisions on preset criteria. Thinkers are extremely concerned about making the right decision.

Feelers, by contrast, make decisions based on their personal values. They tend to focus less on objective criteria and more on how important the decision is to them or to others. They are more concerned than thinkers about the impact the decision is likely to have on others.

Most of us, of course, are a combination of these styles, but we tend to lean in one direction or the other. That tendency can be put to use in sales. If I were selling to someone whom I had identified as a thinker, I would make it a point to present as many hard facts as I could. I would also try to be as logical and structured as I could.

If I were selling to someone whom I had identified as a feeler, I would be much more people-oriented in my approach. I would try to be much more sensitive to the values of the customer.

The MBTI model works. Like any tool, you have to get comfortable with it, practice it, and learn to use it without being too obtrusive. Several good books on MBTI can be found in the psychology section of your library or bookstore. (My personal favorite is *Gifts Differing* by Isabel Briggs Meyers.) And several organizations, including Tennessee Associates International (800-426-4121), have qualified MBTI experts, who can provide on-site testing and interpretation for your organization.

If you would like more information about MBTI, or would like to take the Meyers-Briggs Type Indicator, you can do so by getting in touch with the Association for Psychological Type, 9140 Ward Parkway, Kansas City, Missouri 64114. Telephone: 816-444-3500.

33

THE COMPLEX SALE
When in Rome

MAJOR PURCHASING DECISIONS in most large companies today are no longer made by a single person but require a buy-in from several people. The people involved in the purchase frequently have different jobs and do not always have parallel agendas. The challenge to you in these situations, usually referred to as "*complex sales*," is to tailor your presentation so that all the people involved in the buying decision are convinced that *their* particular concerns are being addressed.

I find it useful in these situations to divide the buyers into three broad categories—and to vary my approach according to which category of person I am trying to sell. Here, in a very broad sense, are the categories and the best approach to take in each instance.

Top-Level Decision Makers With few exceptions, top-level decision makers are motivated primarily by profit. It could be either long-term or short-term profit, but it is always profit. Whenever you are trying to sell a product or service to this group, your focus should be bottom-line: what your product or service is going to do for the company's profit or productivity.

Administrative Staff As a rule, administrative personnel are specification-oriented, and they often feel a need to protect their professional turf. In addition, they are not usually comfortable with change. Their main concern is not necessarily how good your product or service is, but how closely it falls within their departmental standards and specifications. When you are selling to this group, you need to be sensitive to their need for control and sensitive to their reluctance to make changes. The benefit that frequently appeals the most to this group is an easing of their administrative burden.

End Users End users (in many instances, line managers) are mainly interested in how the product or service is going to work for them. They are frequently the most technically knowledgeable of all the groups you work with, and their needs are highly specific, and hands-on.

You need to be especially careful in large, complex corporate settings to involve *everybody* in the buying decision, making sure to give each buyer equal time and attention and to give people in each group a compelling reason to buy—based on *their* needs. Keep in mind that in a complex sale, it takes only one less-than-enthusiastic buyer to produce a hung jury—and a lost sale.

34

CUSTOMER SATISFACTION IS CONTAGIOUS

O NE OF THE BEST—and, in some ways, one of the easiest—ways to convert a prospect into a customer is to make strategic use of your satisfied customers. See if you can arrange a conversation between the prospect and one or more of your most satisfied customers. Let your satisfied customers do the selling job.

I believe so strongly in the power of customer testimonials that I have set up hundreds of such conversations—and have almost always been happy with the results. In most cases, I have had the prospect and the customer talk by phone. Occasionally, though, when I was sure the visit would not create a burden for my customer, I have escorted the prospect to the customer's place of business and then excused myself at the appropriate time to allow the prospect to ask questions and feel that candid answers would be given.

I am also a strong believer in the power of testimonial letters. When customers tell me how happy they are with one of my products or with some special service that I provided, I ask them if they wouldn't mind expressing that satisfaction in writing. I then incorporate such letters into a deluxe loose-leaf binder and use them in my presentations. I've also made it a practice throughout my career to take photographs of my products being used. Those photographs, in and of themselves, are great testimonials.

It's great to have a lot of satisfied customers. It's even better if you can recruit those satisfied customers into your selling strategy.

35

PERFECT TIMING
When to Ask for the Order

ONE OF THE FIRST QUESTIONS I asked when I began my sales career was: "What's the best time during a presentation to ask for the order?" I have never forgotten the answer I received from the man I asked. "Too soon and too often," he said, "is better than too seldom and too late."

At some point in any sales call, regardless of how low-keyed you want to keep things, you have to ask for the business. Knowing *when* to ask the question boils down to something best described as *timing*.

Nobody is born with the sense of timing that tells you at what precise point in your presentation you should be asking for the order—and when it works to your advantage to back off entirely and not ask at all. Looking back, I realize that I probably took that "too soon and too often" advice a little too literally, and, as a result, probably lost sales early in my career because I pushed too hard too soon. Yet, I learned from those mistakes, mainly because I was lucky enough to have mentors and senior managers who coached me.

One obvious key to good timing in sales is paying attention. If you visit a customer when he or she is having a bad day, you are not going to rescue the customer by asking for an order. You need to be able to sense the sort of day someone is having, which means bearing in mind the old Dale Carnegie principle of recognizing that *your* agenda is secondary to the *customer's* agenda.

No one can *teach* you how to improve your sense of timing, but it is something you can learn on your own—just as long as you are willing to make some mistakes and to learn from those mistakes.

36

WHY NO IS A WORD YOU NEVER HAVE TO FEAR

ONE EVENING, I WAS HAVING DINNER with one of my senior salespeople in Kalamazoo, Michigan. As part of a role-play exercise, I said to him, "Jim, sell me on our franchise."

Jim paused for a moment, and then began to

talk. And talk. And talk. Nearly a half-hour later, I interrupted him and said in desperation, "Jim, why didn't you ask me if I was *interested* in the franchise?"

"Because," he said, "I thought you'd say no."

I was fortunate in my career to learn a simple lesson early on: not to be afraid of getting a *no* answer. A *no* answer doesn't end a sale. It merely marks the beginning of a new and separate stage of the process.

A corollary to this principle is that every objection is, in fact, an opportunity—a request for more information. Resistance is neither a sign to quit, nor an invitation to argue. It's the true first step of the sales process.

Here are some of the ways to capitalize on this opportunity.

1 **Agree** The first principle of handling objections is to agree. This principle goes against our natural tendency to argue with an objection. But arguing doesn't work. It tends to put people on the defensive and, if anything, hardens their position. The better way is to agree with the objection. Agreeing with people tends to disarm them.

It takes practice and discipline to break the habit of responding to an objection with a rebuttal. Here are some phrases you can use to help you make the break:

"I understand how you feel . . ."

"I appreciate your point of view . . ."

"You make a good point . . ."

"You are certainly right about . . ."

2 Probe Before you can overcome an objection, you need to understand what exactly you are overcoming. The only way to find this out is to look beyond the objection itself and try to find out the reasons behind it.

Never assume anything. Too many sales are lost because "smart" salespeople think they know the answer when, in fact, they don't even understand the question.

What follows are some basic probing techniques for handling objections.

- *Ask a reflective question.* A reflective question is merely a restatement of the objection, but with an inflection that makes it a question. Objection: "Your price is too high." Reflective question response: "Too *high?*" This simple restatement serves to keep lines of communication open and quietly asks for more information.
- *Ask an open question.* An open question is one that can't be answered with a simple *yes* or *no*: It requires explanation and clarification. If the customer objects to the price, for instance, you can respond with an open question: "I can understand why you might feel that way. Just to clarify my thinking, would you tell me in what way you think our price is too high?"
- *Change the focus.* In this technique, you acknowledge an objection and convert it to a different measure. Here again, if the prospect objects to price, he is often thinking only of original investment. To change the focus, change the frame of reference from original investment to cost over time. In other words,

"scope down"—show how little your product or service costs in the long run.

3 "Brag Up" the Objection This technique, more difficult to use than the others, turns an objection into a reason for buying: Example: A prospect says she has never heard of your company. You agree, but then explain that the reason your company has been successful is that it has focused on satisfying customers and not on advertising. (Note: If you want this technique to work, however, you need to offer some documentation to back up your counterclaim. In this case, you might want to offer a list of references.)

4 Similar Situation After agreeing with the objection, find a similar situation in which another customer had voiced the same concern, and explain how that customer was happy with your product or service.

5 Learn What the Customer Wants to "Think Over" When customers tell you that they want to think things over, it's a good idea to find out why they're hesitating. Go through a list of possibilities of why the customer isn't buying. For example, "What do you want to think over? Is it delivery dates?" or "Is it the product specifications," and so on. Do not pause between "What do you want to think over?" and the first suggestion. If you do, the customer may respond, "The whole thing." Be sure to make price the last suggestion. The rationale behind making price the last possibility you cite is that if you can satisfy the customer on all the other points, price will most likely disappear as an objection.

37

"CAN YOU CUT YOUR PRICE?"—A FABLE

WAY BACK AT THE BEGINNING OF TIME, a great sheik called Al Sta Shun Air owned a herd of donkeys. Sheiks for miles around would come to marvel at the herd. One day, even the Prophet himself, the wisest and most learned son of the East, came to see this herd of donkeys.

With much pride, Al Sta Shun Air led him out to the herd and said, "O Prophet, test these wise and talented asses. Ask of them any question, and they will answer it."

The Prophet said, "What is the fair price for a three-day journey?"

The asses counseled among themselves and said, "O Prophet, the fair price for a three-day journey is five bundles of hay and five bags of dates."

"Good," said the Prophet, "that sounds like a fair and proper price."

Al Sta Shun Air jumped with glee and said, "O Prophet, did I not tell you that these asses are wiser than forty trees full of owls?"

The Prophet said, "Wait, I have need of a three-day journey and I do not need all of you wise asses. Which of you will go for less?"

And behold, they all stood forth and one would go for four bundles of hay and two bags of dates, and another for less, and still another for less. Until finally, one particularly long-eared ass said that he would go on a three-day journey for one bundle of hay.

"Fool!" said the Prophet, "why would you go for three days for one bundle of hay when you can't live for three days on one bundle of hay, much less profit from the journey?"

"That's true," said the long-eared one, "but I wanted the order."

And ever since then, asses have been known as fools and price-cutters have been known as asses.

—Source unknown

38

SELL THE DIFFERENCE

WHEN MY WIFE AND I WERE EXPECTING our first child many years ago, we went shopping for a crib and found ourselves trying to choose between two models in two different stores. One of the cribs sold for $60. The one we eventually bought sold for $85.

We hadn't intended to spend $85 for a crib, but the salesperson was able to demonstrate to us that the $85 was not only a lot sturdier than the one at $60, but also much simpler to assemble and reassemble, which meant we could move it easily from room to room. "You're getting an awful lot for the extra twenty-five dollars," he told us.

What that crib salesman did on that day many years ago is something that successful salespeople do routinely whenever they run into an objection related to price. He didn't make the sale by trying to persuade us to spend $85 for a crib. He made the sale by persuading us to spend $25 more than we had originally intended to spend. He sold us on the "difference."

"Sell the difference" is the most effective response to any objection related to price. When prospects tell you that they like your product or service but that yours is more "expensive" than another they are considering, your next step is to find out who or what they are using as a basis of comparison.

Let's say the price for the service you are offering is $600, and you learn that your competitor's price is $100 less. Your task at this point is simple: You have to sell the *value* to the customer of spending the extra $100.

One of the arguments I often use when I am in this situation is to emphasize to my prospects that if the product or service they are thinking of buying doesn't do what they need it to do, they've lost the entire investment. If they pay "too much," on the other hand, the only real cost to them is the additional money they have spent.

39

HOW TO MAKE NOISE WITH SILENCE

WHENEVER YOU ASK A BUYING QUESTION and you don't get a response, let silence work in your favor.

Inexperienced salespeople frequently fail to do this: They often succumb to the common temptation of trying to fill the silence. They make not-too-bright comments, such as, "Perhaps, you don't like the _____ ."

What this response does, of course, is give the customer an out. Given that out, the customer will usually respond with something like, "That's it." Now, if you want to salvage the sale, you not only have more selling to do, you have to sell from weakness.

When, by contrast, you ask a buying question and then shut up, prospects can do only one of two things: They can agree to buy, or they can raise an objection. If they agree to buy, you're home free. If they raise an objection, you can shift into a different gear and address the objection.

One of the things I never stop stressing to every salesperson I have ever trained is this no-exceptions rule: After you have asked the closing question, keep your mouth *shut*. I can recall dozens of joint calls in which I could sense that the person I was training was bursting at the seams to break the uncomfortable silence that followed the question. Afterward, we had something to chuckle over. We knew the rule, and neither of us dared break the silence. There is no pressure in selling that equals the pressure of silence after asking a closing question.

40

JUMPING THE GUN
The Assumptive Close

WHENEVER YOU'RE DEALING WITH A CUSTOMER who is on the verge of saying *yes* but hasn't actually given you the go-ahead, you can frequently get the result you want by employing an old—but usually reliable—technique known as the assumptive close.

The way it works is this: Instead of coming out and asking the closing question directly, you ask a question that presupposes a *yes* answer to the closing question. Example: "When do you want delivery: on Tuesday or Wednesday?"

The main thing to be careful about when using this technique is making sure the customer is receptive to it. If you try this presumptive approach too early in the process, your customers may see it as a form of pressure, and the tactic might backfire.

The assumptive close is important in those situations in which a customer has asked for time to make up his mind, and you have now come back to the customer to get the final answer.

The natural tendency in a situation like this is to open with a question like, "Well, have you thought it over?" This question, though, is an invitation for the customer to voice a misgiving or objection. You are much better off acting as if the answer is going to be yes, and move smoothly into the order-writing process as soon as you've gotten past the preliminaries. Doing so puts customers in the position of having to interrupt you if they aren't yet ready to buy.

One of the best retail-clothing salespeople I know swears by what she calls the "Which do you prefer?" technique. If she has a customer interested in, say, a tie, she will show several and quickly narrow the selection down to two or three, at which point she will ask directly: "Which do you prefer, the plaid or the stripe?"

A standard order form, presented at the appropriate time, can also be a powerful assumptive close, provided it is presented in a routine, almost nonchalant way. Once the customer has indicated that he or she is about to say yes, you start the paperwork. You begin by asking the correct full name, then the address, etc. The more information the customer gives you, the closer you are to a true close.

41

HELPING PROSPECTS GET OVER THE FENCE

WHENEVER BENJAMIN FRANKLIN HAD A DECISION TO MAKE, he would take a sheet of plain paper and draw a line down the middle. He would put *Yes* over the left-hand column and *No* over the right-hand column. He would then list all the reasons why he should and shouldn't make the decision, and compare the two lists.

I have described this process to hundreds of customers who were on the fence, and in many cases, have actually given them a sheet of paper to help them through the process.

I begin by saying, "Let's think of all of the reasons why we *should* do this," and I coach the customer through the *yes* list. When that list is complete, I ask the customer to list the *no* reasons, except that this time, I don't offer any help. I leave it up to customers to supply the reasons they shouldn't buy.

What usually happens is that the customer is unable to come with enough *no* reasons to overcome the number of *yes* reasons.

42

WHY NOBODY EVER RETURNS PUPPIES

SUPPOSE THAT OVER YOUR SPOUSE'S STRENUOUS OBJECTIONS, you brought home a puppy for the kids. "Here's the deal I made with the pet shop," you say. "We can return the puppy anytime for up to a week and get all our money back."

After a week (assuming your kids are like most kids when it comes to puppies), what are the chances that the puppy is ever going back to the pet shop? Virtually nonexistent, I think you would agree.

Letting your customers sample one of your products or services before they actually commit is one of the oldest techniques in selling, but it works just as well today as it did fifty years ago. If the product is any good at all, they won't want to part with it.

In the days when washing machines weren't too common, an old friend, Martin Trout, would stop by a neighborhood where he knew a lot of people, pay a visit to a homeowner, and offer to leave a washing machine for a demonstration. "No purchase necessary," Trout would say. "I just have to get one more on demonstration to make my quota for the month."

Trout would wait a few weeks and return to the neighborhood. He wouldn't go directly to the house of the person where he'd left the washing machine. He would go instead to the house of a neighbor for a cup of coffee. During the conversation with the neighbor, Trout would mention that he was on his way to pick up a demonstrator he had left next door. If he got no response, he would continue to leave the model out on demo. But if the neighbor said, "Oh, I don't think you'll need to pick it up. They want to keep it," Trout would go next door to pick up his "demonstrator."

When he was greeted at the door, he would say hello and announce in a friendly way that he had come to pick up the machine. He would then start to move toward the basement, but he rarely got very far. Indeed, before he got to the door of the basement, he would usually be told by the prospect what he already knew—that the homeowner wanted to keep the machine.

Trout proved with his technique that you can make a sale without having to ask for the order—and without lowering your price.

43

HOLD SOMETHING BACK

H AS THIS EVER HAPPENED TO you?
You are browsing in a second-hand store, and you see a table that catches your eye. The price tag on the table reads $300. You go to the owner and say, "I'll give you two hundred and fifty," and the owner, without blinking an eye, says, "Great, you have a deal."

Presumably, you should be happy. After all,

you've bought something you wanted at *your* price. What bothers you, though, is how quickly the owner jumped at your offer. You are haunted by the suspicion that you could have probably bought the table for a good deal less. You now experience what is commonly referred to as "buyer's remorse."

Let's change the scenario. Let's say when you offer the owner $250, the owner looks shocked and offended. "That table originally sold for more than a thousand dollars," the owner tells you. "It's already priced as low as I can price it." Ten minutes later, after negotiating back and forth, you settle on a price: $275. That's $25 more than you paid in the first scenario. Yet, you walk away feeling as though you've picked up one of the bargains of the century.

The lesson to be learned here is this. Whenever you are in any sales negotiating situation with a customer, always know before you enter the negotiation what you are prepared to offer, but don't be in too much of a hurry to offer it or agree to it. Once you know what you are prepared to offer, the only issue that remains is how happy the customer is going to be when you eventually "give in."

The selling principle just described might strike you as a form of gamesmanship that is incompatible with the philosophy of "getting married" to the customer, as I have been preaching throughout this book. It's not. Even married people need to negotiate with each other from time to time, and not giving in right away on a point you know you'll eventually concede is an acceptable tactic—as long you do it in the right spirit. As important as it is to serve your customers in the best way you know how, it is just as important to gain their appreciation.

There is corollary to the principle I have just

described. I call it the "If I can do it, will you . . ." approach.

The way it works is this: When a prospect asks you if you are willing to make certain concessions, or to modify your offer, you can usually interpret this response as a buying signal, but you need to weigh your response carefully. The correct answer, regardless of what you are being asked, is neither *yes* nor *no*. It should be, "If I can do this, will you (commit)?"

Assuming you already know that you can fulfill the request, the "If I can do it, will you . . ." approach is a great way to close the close. Even if the buyer agrees that fulfilling the request will indeed result in a sale, it is still a good idea to withhold your response. As I've already mentioned, giving in too quickly to a buyer's request creates that all-too-familiar disease sometimes referred to as buyer's remorse—the feeling that if the customer had asked for more, he would have gotten a better deal.

The "If I can do it, will you . . ." technique works best when you, as seller, know ahead of time that the request can be fulfilled. But you can also use it when you need to get approval from a higher authority, albeit with this caveat: only if you are reasonably sure you can get the authority.

44

TIP THE SCALES IN THE CUSTOMER'S FAVOR

S EVERAL YEARS AGO, after completing a tour of a silver mine in Colorado, I decided to buy a dollar's worth of silver from the old prospector who had conducted the tour.

The prospector got out a set of balance scales and placed a silver dollar on one side. This caused the empty side to tip upward. Then he began pouring silver dust on the empty platform. When the two sides of the scale were evenly balanced, I knew I had a dollar's worth of silver dust.

The prospector didn't stop. He kept pouring on the silver dust until that side of the scale was tipped way over in my favor. I knew then that I had much more than a dollar's worth. A real value! I walked away a happy customer.

Conventional wisdom would suggest that giving something extra to the customer *after* you've made a sale is a foolish move. This prospector, however, knew otherwise, and so should you. Here's why:

Whenever most people make a key buying decision—especially if the decision has been difficult to reach—they tend to experience a certain amount of anxiety over whether they made the right decision. If, in the aftermath of the sale, something occurs (or doesn't occur) that feeds the doubt, a customer is likely to reconsider the decision and, in some cases, might experience a change of heart. But, should something happen that reinforces the wisdom of the decision, the doubt and the anxiety are greatly eased.

The obvious message: Even after the customer has said *yes*, look for ways to tip the scale way over with a full measure of benefits.

PART V

MAKING
THE CUSTOMER
YOUR PARTNER

45

MIND YOUR CUSTOMER'S BUSINESS

I F YOU ARE MARRIED, the welfare of your spouse is inseparable from your own welfare. Successful sales relationships are no different. The more you do to make your customers successful, the more success you are likely to enjoy.

The late Charles Revson, founder of Revlon, built one of the world's most powerful corporations in America by emphasizing a selling concept usually referred to as the "sell-through." As Revson saw it, Revlon's responsibility to its retailers didn't end when the order arrived in the customers' stores. It was also up to Revlon—and in Revlon's best interests—to do everything in its power to help retailers sell Revlon products to *their* customers. Among other things, Revlon helped to pioneer the concept of a "beauty advisor"—a cosmetic specialist who worked at the Revlon counter in the retailer's store, but was actually on Revlon's payroll.

Before you can begin to help your customers become more successful, you need to understand their business. This means you have to take an interest in that business. My method of incorporating this principle into my selling strategy is to spend at least part of every sales call talking about the customer's overall business—not merely the part of the business that relates to what I'm selling. It helps immeasurably, by the way, to have a genuine and healthy curiosity about your customer's business and what makes it tick.

If you are faithful to the principle of minding your customer's business, you may occasionally find yourself—as I have on many occasions—trying to strike a balance between satisfying a customer's need and desire and staying within the guidelines that have been set by your own company. Being able to strike this balance becomes more difficult, of course, as the gap between what your customers *want* and what your company *allows* becomes wider and wider, but even when the gap is narrow, the balancing act can be tricky.

I wish there were an easy way out of this common quandary, but there isn't. The challenge to you, as someone in the middle, is to keep the lines of communication open on both ends. You owe it your customers to set up the arrangements that are the most advantageous to them. At the same time, you can't expect to run roughshod over your company's own policies—not unless you own the company.

Different sales professionals I have known through the years have handled this problem in different ways. One acquaintance who sells different lines for a variety of manufacturers negotiates vigorously with each company he represents for the right to tailor company policies on payment terms, delivery charges, returns, and such to individual customers. In some cases, he gives up a percentage of his commission to gain a concession, but he has found that what he might lose in commission, he more than makes up by doing larger volume.

I also know many sales reps who have managed to persuade the companies whose products and services they sell that certain company policies—particularly those that were arbitrarily established years before—are simply bad business and need to be changed in order to keep the company competitive.

In any case, there are two things you can do to avoid the pressure and the problems that arise when you are forced to strike the balance I am describing here.

The first thing is to make sure that you are thoroughly familiar not only with your *own* company's policies, but with the policies of your competitors as well. Knowing what concessions your customers can expect to get if they were to take their business elsewhere gives you an important edge in any negotiation.

What you need to be especially careful about doing is promising what you can't—or are not authorized to—offer. I have found throughout my career that the decision makers in the companies whose products and services I have sold are flexible about policies, providing there is a strong rationale for making exceptions. What the policy makers *don't* like, however, is the feeling that they are being backed into a corner—especially by somebody in their own company.

46

BE EASY TO REACH

W HEN I CALLED MY OFFICE TO RETRIEVE my messages a few days ago, I learned that one of my new customers had called me only fifteen minutes earlier. As is my practice, I returned the call immediately, and was surprised at how grateful the customer was that I had returned the call so promptly. It occurred to me as we were speaking that this simple gesture in and of itself—returning calls promptly—had already given me an edge over my competitors.

Customers—particularly big customers—like to work with salespeople who are easy to get hold of. That's a given in business. If you are easy to reach, you will usually outperform salespeople who are difficult to reach.

Think for a moment. If one of your key customers has a problem, how easy or difficult is it for the customer to get you on the phone? How many times, for instance, will the phone ring at your place of business before it is answered? And what will happen next? Will the person who answers the phone recognize the customer's name, or will the customer get the third degree: Name? Company? Reason for call? Professional affiliation? Blood type?

And what if you're not in your office? Are you easy to get hold of (and in this era of cellular phones and beepers, there is no excuse for *not* being easy to reach!), or is the customer automatically routed to your voice mail? Voice mail may be one of the great conveniences of twentieth-century communication, but it can be an inconvenience and a nuisance to your customers. If you have voice mail, how frequently do you call to retrieve your messages?

Making it easy for customers to reach you is common sense. But because this common sense is not commonly followed, following it can give you a significant competitive edge.

47

MAKE YOURSELF INDISPENSABLE

I F YOU RESENT IT WHEN YOUR CUSTOMERS make special demands, you're probably in the wrong line of work. If anything, you should consider yourself lucky when you find yourself with a good customer who needs special treatment. It's one more way to be of service—an additional way to cement the relationship by becoming indispensable.

A young woman I know who has become exceptionally successful selling printing services is a striking illustration of my point. Many of her clients are small businesses run by people who do not have the staff resources to double-check the copy they submit for brochures and ads. She makes it her business to read and reread everything her customers want printed, and more often than not, she finds little errors that would have proven embarrassing if they had not been detected. You can imagine how grateful her customers are whenever she uncovers these errors. If I were selling printing services, I would not want to have this woman as a competitor.

48

BUILD FRIENDSHIPS

I MENTIONED MUCH EARLIER IN THE BOOK that the personal relationship you develop with the people you are trying to sell is no longer as important a factor in selling success as it once was. Once you have *established* a selling relationship with a customer, however, the personal side of that relationship remains as important as ever. Everything else being equal, people prefer to buy from people they like. The more your customers view you as a friend, the more likely they are to remain a customer—just as long as your product or service continues to meet their needs.

Some people have a problem with the notion of becoming friends with their customers, but I don't share this view. On the contrary, becoming friends with my customers has made the selling I do not only easier, but a lot more enjoyable. I look forward to many of the sales calls I make with the same anticipation I would feel if I were meeting with a good friend I hadn't seen for a while. I win both ways.

How do you turn a customer into a friend? Just as you would make a friend out of anyone. You find common ground (kids or a subject or cause you both care about, for example). You show concern for the person. You stay in touch. You make it a point to be there if the person needs help. The message you always want to convey is that "even though we know each other through business, I value your friendship."

One obvious way to turn customers into friends is to create social situations for your customers. When I visit another city, I call people with whom I would like to strengthen a friendship and invite them to breakfast, lunch, or dinner. Even if the invitation is declined, it still strengthens the relationship.

One more thing: Should a customer who has become a friend lose his or her job, do your best to keep that friendship alive and try to be as helpful as you can as that person tries to find another job. The obvious reason—apart from the fact that it is the decent thing to do—is that people who were customers when they were working for one company are likely to become your customers in their new jobs.

49

BE AVAILABLE WHEN THINGS GO WRONG

W HAT SOME SALESPEOPLE do when a customer runs into a problem is lie low until the storm blows over. Either that, or they look to somebody else in the company to solve the problem. That is a big mistake.

You don't get many opportunities to be a hero in a sales relationship. When things are going well, customers tend to take you for granted. The best way to be appreciated is to be there when a problem arises, and meet the problem head on.

Interestingly enough, whether or not you actually *solve* a customer's problem is not nearly as important as simply being there to listen as the customer describes the problem. Your empathy and efforts, in other words, frequently count as much as the results you are able to obtain.

A study published a few years ago by Abt Associates of Cambridge, Massachusetts, turned up some interesting data. It showed a direct correlation between customer dissatisfaction and the number of people the customer had to talk to before the problem was fixed. Another study by Abt, though, showed that when customers received answers to mail inquiries within ten days, they were much more likely to be satisfied with the response, *regardless of the response*.

Here again the lesson is clear. The main thing most dissatisfied customers want is to know that somebody cares and is paying attention to the problem.

An experience a friend of mine recently had during a stay at the Oriental Hotel in Tokyo proves my point. His office advised him that a fax had been sent several hours before, but it wasn't until he called the front desk that the fax was delivered. My friend was not pleased, but the next day, he was called by the assistant manager, who not only apologized profusely for the delay but insisted on doing something extra to make amends. Because the hotel showed genuine concern, the Oriental is the only hotel my friend stays in when he visits Tokyo.

Another friend, a man who manages a chain of shirt shops, helped to produce a marked increase in sales by making a small change in the company's complaints procedure. The company's policy always had been to investigate each complaint and offer an adjustment based on the merit of the complaint. Under the new policy, *every* complaint was answered *immediately*, and each response included an apology and a small gift.

Have you stopped to think about what you do in your company whenever a customer has a problem? How many people, for instance, does a customer have to talk to before that problem is resolved? And what happens after the problem has been reported?

The five simple steps that follow ought to be a fixed part of your customer-dissatisfaction policy. As you read this list, think about how closely the steps mirror what happens in your company when a customer has a problem.

1. Respond immediately.
2. Apologize.
3. Ask what you can do to correct the situation.
4. Take action.
5. Offer a value-added atonement.

50

LITTLE THINGS THAT MEAN A LOT

I HAVE HAD THE GOOD FORTUNE in my career to build dozens of successful, long-term sales relationships. One of the main reasons I have been able to do so is that I have gone out of my way to do little things that let my customers know how much I appreciate their business.

To begin with, I make it my business to become aware of the special concerns a customer might have in connection with any specific situation, and I go out of my way to ease those concerns. If I know that a customer is particularly anxious about getting a shipment by a certain date, I will make it a point to call, just to reassure the customer that everything is going according to plan.

I also make it my business to learn as much as I can about the personal lives of my customers. I keep track of their birthdays and anniversary dates. I write down the names of their family members. It makes a big difference to ask, "How are Danny and Susan?" instead of "How are your children doing?"

I'm interested in knowing what interests my customers: their hobbies, the sports they play, the books they read, the kind of traveling they like to do. Being able to open a conversation by talking about any of these areas of interest is a great way to reestablish a connection if I haven't spoken to a customer for a long time. If I come across a magazine article about a subject a customer is interested in, I can clip and send it—a gesture that takes small effort but generates lots of goodwill.

I'm also a big believer in sending cards and gifts, although the gifts I give are never lavish or expensive. If I call on a customer during Secretaries Week, I take a small gift to his or her secretary. On Halloween, I take a box of candy to offices I call on.

Another thing I do that most salespeople don't do is send Thanksgiving cards. Why? Because Thanksgiving cards stand out from the clutter and invariably get a better reaction than Christmas cards, which most people take for granted. It is amazing how many people make it a point to tell me how much they enjoy and appreciate my Thanksgiving cards.

My purpose in all of this is simple: to make my customers feel special and let them know in small ways that I don't take their business for granted.

ABOUT THE AUTHOR

Gerald A. Michaelson has been a highly successful sales and marketing professional for more than thirty years, during which time he has held a variety of positions, ranging from independent sales representative to national sales vice president of a Fortune 500 company. He is currently executive vice president of Tennessee Associates International of Knoxville, where his specialty is working with managers throughout the world to create high-performance organizations. Mr. Michaelson is author of the acclaimed *Winning the Marketing War* (described by *Success* magazine as "The best book on strategy ever written"). Formerly national vice president of the American Marketing Association, he writes a regular column for *Success* and has been a contributing editor to *Sales & Marketing Management*.